WITHDRAWN

FOOTBALL'S
GREATEST
STARS

PEYTON MANNING

by Matt Scheff

SportsZone

An Imprint of Abdo Publishing
abdopublishing.com

abdopublishing.com

Published by Abdo Publishing, a division of ABDO, PO Box 398166, Minneapolis, Minnesota 55439. Copyright © 2016 by Abdo Consulting Group, Inc. International copyrights reserved in all countries. No part of this book may be reproduced in any form without written permission from the publisher. SportsZone™ is a trademark and logo of Abdo Publishing.

Printed in the United States of America, North Mankato, Minnesota
042015
092015

THIS BOOK CONTAINS
RECYCLED MATERIALS

Cover Photos: Eric Bakke/AP Images (foreground); Charlie Riedel/AP Images (background)
Interior Photos: Eric Bakke/AP Images, 1 (foreground); Charlie Riedel/AP Images, 1 (background); Alex Brandon/AP Images, 4-5; Jeff Roberson/AP Images, 6-7; Ed Bailey/AP Images, 8; Mark Humphrey/AP Images, 9, 14, 15; Bettmann/Corbis, 10-11; Scott Audette/AP Images, 12-13; Kevin Terrell/AP Images, 16-17; G. Newman Lowrance/AP Images, 18-19; Michael Conroy/AP Images, 20-21; Ben Liebenberg/AP Images, 22-23; David Zalubowski/AP Images, 24-25, 26-27; Jack Dempsey/AP Images, 28-29

Editor: Nick Rebman
Series Designer: Jake Nordby

Library of Congress Control Number: 2015932400

Cataloging-in-Publication Data
Scheff, Matt.
 Peyton Manning / Matt Scheff.
   p. cm. -- (Football's greatest stars)
Includes index.
ISBN 978-1-62403-826-6
1. Manning, Peyton--Juvenile literature. 2. Football players--United States--Biography--Juvenile literature. 3. Quarterbacks (Football)--United States--Biography--Juvenile literature.   I. Title.
796.332092--dc23
[B]   2015932400

CONTENTS

THE BIGGEST GAME

The 2007 Super Bowl started badly for quarterback Peyton Manning and the Indianapolis Colts. Devin Hester of the Chicago Bears returned the opening kickoff for a touchdown. Then the Colts got the ball, and Manning threw an interception.

Manning was one of the league's top passers. Yet he had struggled in past playoff games. Did he have the talent to win the biggest game of all?

FAST FACT
Manning entered the 2006 season with a playoff record of just 3-6.

Manning and his teammates huddle in the rain during the 2007 Super Bowl.

Manning calls a play as the rain comes down during the Super Bowl.

On the Colts' next possession, Manning threw downfield to receiver Reggie Wayne. Wayne caught the ball and darted into the end zone. Touchdown!

That was just the beginning. Manning's pinpoint passing combined with the Colts' powerful running attack. Even a steady rain and a tough Bears defense could not stop Indianapolis. The Colts were champions!

FAST FACT
Manning was named the Most Valuable Player (MVP) of the 2007 Super Bowl.

FOOTBALL FAMILY

Peyton Manning was born on March 24, 1976, in New Orleans, Louisiana. Peyton had football in his blood. His father, Archie, was a star quarterback in the National Football League (NFL). Peyton and his older brother, Cooper, began throwing footballs to each other when they were toddlers. Later, their younger brother Eli joined in the fun. The three brothers loved to compete with each other.

Peyton Manning, *right*, poses with his father, *left*, and brother Eli, *center*.

Manning runs the ball as a Georgia defender chases him.

FAST FACT
Archie Manning played for the New Orleans Saints, the Houston Oilers, and the Minnesota Vikings during his 13-year NFL career.

Manning, *right,* meets with
Tennessee coach Phil Fulmer during
a 1997 game against Florida.

Peyton took over as his high
school's starting quarterback as
a sophomore. His brother Cooper
was his favorite receiver. Two years
later, Peyton threw 39 touchdown
passes as a senior. Colleges all
around the country wanted him to
join their teams.

Many fans expected Peyton
to attend his father's school,
the University of Mississippi. But
Peyton accepted a scholarship to
Tennessee.

FAST FACT
Cooper and Eli both
went to the University
of Mississippi. However,
a serious spinal condition
kept Cooper from ever
playing football there.

VOLUNTEER

Manning did not expect to play much for the Tennessee Volunteers as a freshman in 1994. But he soon became the starter. Manning's accuracy and decision-making were far beyond his years. He led the team to a Gator Bowl victory.

Manning was even better in 1995. The Volunteers lost only one game all season. Then they won the Citrus Bowl and finished the season ranked third in the nation.

FAST FACT

Manning was named the Southeastern Conference Freshman of the Year in 1994.

Manning had great numbers during his junior year. Many experts said he could be the top pick in the upcoming NFL Draft. But Manning made a surprise announcement. He said he would return to Tennessee for his senior year.

Manning had a great season as a senior. He finished second in the Heisman Trophy voting.

Manning runs onto the field for his final home game with the Tennessee Volunteers.

Manning calls a play during a game against the University of Mississippi in 1997.

FAST FACT
Manning earned his college degree in speech communication.

WELCOME TO THE NFL

Manning was the top prospect in the 1998 NFL Draft. The Colts selected him with the first pick. But Manning's rookie year was rough. He threw a league-high 28 interceptions, and the Colts went just 3-13.

Manning improved quickly, though. He led Indianapolis to the playoffs in 1999 and 2000. In his third NFL season, he led the league with 33 touchdown passes.

Manning attempts a pass against the San Francisco 49ers during his rookie season in the NFL.

FAST FACT
Manning was named to his first Pro Bowl after the 1999 season.

Manning changes a play at the line of scrimmage during his first MVP season in 2003.

By 2003, many experts considered Manning the NFL's best passer. He was famous for the way he directed the offense with his pointing and loud signal calling. His methods worked. Manning was named the NFL's MVP in 2003 and again in 2004.

Yet Indianapolis could not seem to beat the New England Patriots in the playoffs. New England, led by quarterback Tom Brady, got the best of the Colts in both of those seasons.

FAST FACT

In 2004 Manning set an NFL record by throwing 49 touchdown passes.

SUPERSTAR

In the 2007 AFC Championship Game, it looked like Brady and the Patriots would again defeat the Colts. The Patriots had roared to a 21-3 lead. But then Manning took over. The Colts scored 32 points in the second half to win 38-34. They went on to beat the Bears in the Super Bowl.

FAST FACT

The Colts erased an 18-point deficit in the 2007 AFC title game. It was the biggest comeback ever in a conference championship game.

Manning heaves a pass during the AFC Championship Game against the New England Patriots.

Manning and the Colts enjoyed solid seasons in 2007 and 2008. That included another MVP trophy for Manning in 2008. Yet Indianapolis struggled in the playoffs. In 2009 the Colts went 14-2, and Manning earned his fourth MVP award. More importantly, the Colts returned to the Super Bowl. Manning led his team to an early lead, but Indianapolis lost to the New Orleans Saints 31-17.

Manning passes the ball in the Super Bowl against the New Orleans Saints.

FAST FACT
Peyton's younger brother, Eli, won the Super Bowl in 2008 and 2012 as quarterback of the New York Giants.

Manning had neck pain after a disappointing 2010 season. In 2011 surgeons fused two of the bones in his neck. They said he might never play again. Manning missed the entire 2011 season. Then the Colts released him. Manning was free to sign with any team. In 2012 he picked the Denver Broncos.

FAST FACT

Before the 2011 season, Manning had not missed a single game in his entire NFL career.

Manning, *center*, poses with Broncos owner Pat Bowlen, *left*, and Broncos vice president John Elway, *right*, after signing with the team.

MILE HIGH

At first, Broncos fans wondered if Manning could be the great quarterback he had been before his surgery. Soon they had no doubt. Manning led the Broncos to a 13-3 record in 2012.

It only got better from there. In 2013 Manning won his fifth MVP award. He set an NFL record with 55 touchdown passes. He also led the Broncos to the Super Bowl.

FAST FACT

Manning was named the NFL's 2012 Comeback Player of the Year.

Manning takes a snap during his first game as a member of the Denver Broncos.

Denver looked like the team to beat when the 2014 season began. Manning was on fire. But he struggled late in the season, and the Broncos lost to the Colts in the playoffs.

No matter what Manning's future holds, his legacy is secure. No player in NFL history has thrown more touchdown passes or won more MVP awards. Many argue that he is the greatest quarterback ever to play the game.

FAST FACT
Manning owns more than 20 pizza stores in Colorado.

Manning's teammates congratulate him after he set the all-time record for touchdown passes.

TIMELINE

1976
Peyton Manning is born on March 24 in New Orleans, Louisiana.

1994
Manning accepts a scholarship to Tennessee and takes over as the starting quarterback during his freshman year.

1998
The Indianapolis Colts select Manning with the first pick in the NFL Draft. He starts for the Colts as a rookie.

2003
Manning wins his first NFL MVP award.

2007
The Colts defeat the Chicago Bears in the Super Bowl, and Manning is voted the game's MVP.

2010
Manning and the Colts return to the Super Bowl but lose to the New Orleans Saints.

2012
Manning signs with the Denver Broncos.

2013
Manning wins his fifth NFL MVP award and leads the Broncos to the Super Bowl.

GLOSSARY

ACCURACY
The ability to throw the ball on target.

FUSE
To join together.

HEISMAN TROPHY
An honor given to the top college football player each year.

PROSPECT
A player expected to succeed at the next level of play.

ROOKIE
A first-year player.

SCHOLARSHIP
Money given to a student to pay for education expenses.

SIGNAL CALLING
The act of shouting out play calls and adjustments before a play.

INDEX

ABOUT THE AUTHOR

Matt Scheff is an artist and author living in Alaska. He enjoys
mountain climbing, deep-sea fishing, and curling up with his
two Siberian huskies to watch football.